SANTORINI:

Make your dream come true

CONTENTS

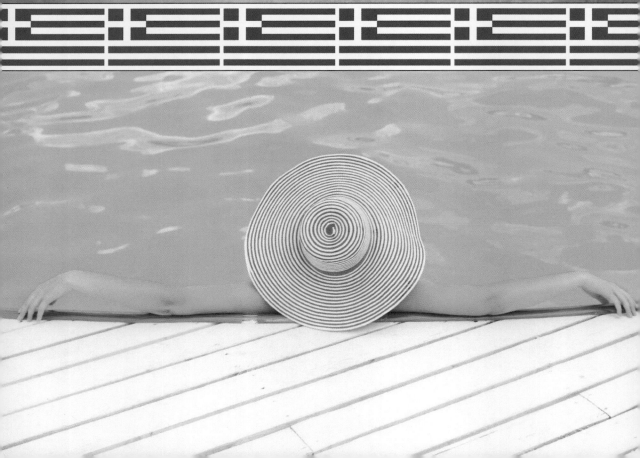

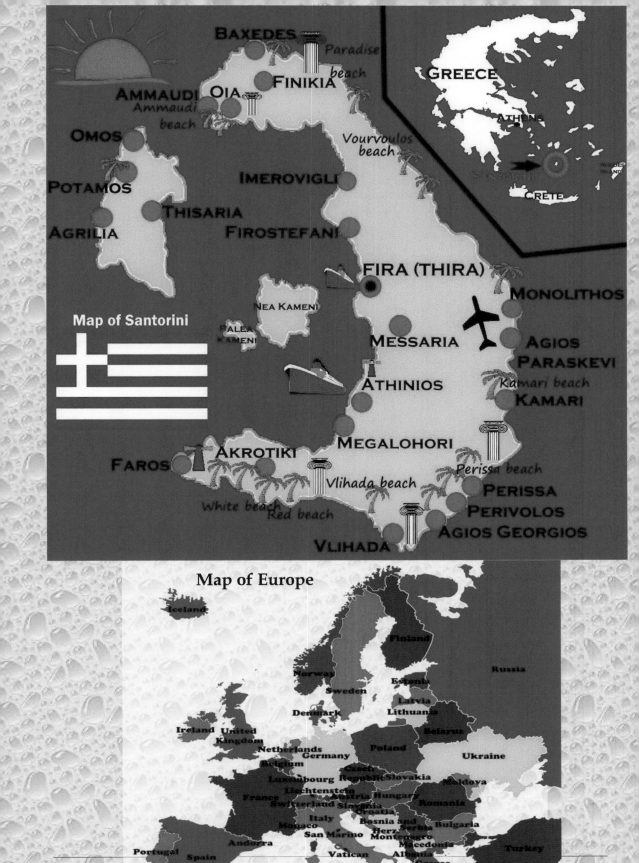

Map of Santorini

BAXEDES
Paradise beach
AMMAUDI
Ammaudi beach
OIA
FINIKIA
OMOS
Vourvoulos beach
POTAMOS
IMEROVIGLI
THISARIA
AGRILIA
FIROSTEFANI
FIRA (THIRA)
NEA KAMENI
MONOLITHOS
PALEA KAMENI
MESSARIA
AGIOS PARASKEVI
Kamari beach
ATHINIOS
KAMARI
FAROS
AKROTIKI
MEGALOHORI
Vlihada beach
Perissa beach
White beach   Red beach
PERISSA
PERIVOLOS
AGIOS GEORGIOS
VLIHADA

GREECE
ATHENS
CRETE
RHODES ISLAND
Santorini

Map of Europe

Iceland
Finland
Norway
Russia
Sweden
Estonia
Denmark
Latvia
Lithuania
Ireland   United Kingdom
Belarus
Netherlands
Germany
Poland
Ukraine
Belgium
Czech Republic
Slovakia
Moldova
Luxembourg
Liechtenstein
Austria   Hungary
France
Switzerland
Slovenia
Romania
Italy
Croatia
Monaco
Bosnia and Herz.
Serbia
Bulgaria
San Marino
Montenegro
Macedonia
Portugal
Andorra
Vatican
Albania
Turkey
Spain
Greece
Malta

3

General reference, major towns (settlements)

Santorini is one of the most mysterious and beautiful islands not only in Greece, but in the whole world! Dozens of legends are associated with its name. Some people say it's Atlantis; others call it Pompeii of the Aegean Sea. These legends have grounds. The island came into existence as a result of a volcanic eruption and this fact determined the fate of the island. There were 12 eruptions during the history of the island's existence, but after every one of them Santorini, like Phoenix, rose from its ashes.

The island is picturesque and captivating! Santorini tops the list of the five most spectacular islands of the world. It is followed by such famous places like Bali in Indonesia and the Great Barrier Reef in Australia. And there are some more comparisons. If Paris is considered to be the most romantic city in the world, then Santorini is considered to be the most romantic among the islands. Like a tender pearl in the crown of the Greek islands, it has become a perfect place for marriages. Couples from all over the world rush to this island to swear an oath of eternal love and leave this place with breathtaking pictures.

Santorini is a group of islands that were formed as a result of a volcanic eruption. Crescent-shaped Fira, Thirassia, Aspronissi, Nea and Palea Kameni are in the center of the depthless caldera. Everything is unique and unusual here. There are colorful beaches with black pebbles, red sand or white volcanic foam. The sea color varies from bright emerald-green to dark blue and almost black.

The water is cool and refreshing as the depth of the sea is up to 400 meters.

Snow-white houses, perched high up on the cliffs, seem to be a white cloud, having descended onto the top of the mountain. They are located so close to each other that the sundeck of one house appears to be the roof of the other.

Steep cliffs of the western shore are changing into endless beaches of the eastern edge of the island. Some of them are sandy covered with dark almost black sand, others are pebbled.

Every tourist is fascinated by the mysteries of ancient civilizations, Cycladic architecture as well as supernatural energy.

FIRA (THIRA)

The capital of Santorini is the town of Fira (Thira), and its upper part, in particular, is a unique and astonishing place. It tops all I have ever seen! This town is considered to be the most authentic in Europe.

The town of Fira chimes in with the outstanding beauty of the island. This toy- town, fairy-like town is located high up on the edge of the caldera. The volcanic eruption has changed the course of the history of the Ancient World. Snow-white houses, chiseled balconies, ways up and down, an endless number of little crooked streets are climbing up the cliff and the houses perched on each other make up the present-day capital of Santorini.

The town of Fira was the capital in Dorian epoch. There are a lot of stormy events in its history such as invaders' rule, natural disasters, earthquakes and nations' shift. But all the same, people returned to this place, rebuilding their astounding town time and again.

The international airport is situated 6 km away from the capital (in the settlement of Kamari). The airport accommodates regular flights from Athens, and in summer it accommodates chartered flights from other cities of Greece and Europe (London, Manchester, Birmingham, Bristol, Newcastle, Barcelona, Paris, Milan, Rome, etc.)

One can get from the airport to the capital of the island by taxi or bus. Lots of tourists come to Santorini in the summer. Almost half a million passengers arrive at the airport during high season for all that the population of the island is about 14,000 people and the population of Fira is only 1,500 people. The population of the island and its capital increases dramatically during high season.

The romantic style of Fira's hotel rooms carved in cliffs is in a perfect harmony with the view over the sea and of sunset.

The major town of Santorini is located high up on the cliff. Fira is the Greek name of the whole island. The name of Santorini was given by crusaders who used to put up at Saint Irene's cathedral.

One can find white toy houses with sapphire or brick-red blinds scattered along the side of the cliff. One of the ports, Messa Gialos, is downwards. It accommodates cruise liners and pleasure-boats.

You can access the town in three ways: by a stairway of 800 stair-steps (it's for trained people), by donkeys (for those who are brave and don't mind some foul smell and jolting, but it is romantic) and by more convenient means – cable car.

Fira is very popular with tourists and that's why it's expensive. Upmarket hotels, designer stores, restaurants, and bars fit into narrow mazes of streets. You can visit a number of museums in Fira.

One of them is the archaeological museum with ancient Fira's artifacts dating back to the Geometric Period. You can admire a rich and interesting collection of exhibit items telling about the history of the island. Among these items are ceramic and copper items, Cycladic marble fetishes,and jewelry.

The ethnographical museum puts up to the daily routine and customs of the locals. You can see furniture, instruments, utensils, handicrafts, folk costumes, and pictures there.

It will be interesting to visit 2 cathedrals – the Orthodox Cathedral and the Catholic Cathedral of Fira, as well as Dominican Convent, Cultural Centre of Gyzi Manor, and St. Min Church with a distinctive sapphire dome, which is an advertising card of the island.

Fira is a place where you can start your tour around the island.

Metropolis St. is the heart of the capital. It's a pedestrianized street named after the church located here. The church is considered to be the most magnificent church of the island.

This top of the capital overlooks the sea reaching the skyline and two black cliffy islands called Kamenos, which means "burnt."

By the way, the unusual taste of local grapes is due to volcanic soil and lack of rain. They have been grown by the locals for 3,500 years. They are called Assyrtiko and are used for making local wine. I'll describe the wines and local cuisine in details in a relevant chapter.

Tour boats depart from the old port of Fira for Thirassia, Nea and Palea Kameni every day.

Thirassia is a small island; its area is 9 square km and its population is 270 people. Its patriarchal structure and silence are in sharp contrast to noisy tourist filled Fira. There are 20 churches and chapels in small settlements scattered on the island.

There are sulfur healing springs on Palea Kameni. Tour boats can't close to the beach, so you can't get there other than by swimming. You should take dark swimsuits if you want to swim in healing springs because the reddish water can soak into fabric for a long time.

The end goal of the tour is Nea Kameni, where you can see the crater of the dormant volcano. You'll have to spend a lot of time and effort to reach its rim. You must have a potable water supply, sunscreen, and appropriate shoes because the sun is scalding and the soil is quite hot.

OIA

The most beautiful and elite village of the island is Oia. Building norms in Oia are observed in the most rigorous way, therefore even new houses correspond to a special Oia variant of the Teclane architecture. A rounded form, white-blue colors, narrow streets paved with stones; and it is also believed that the most impressive view of the sunset is here.

Thousands of people come to watch it every evening! YOU ARE ALSO SIMPLY OBLIGED TO SEE THIS BEAUTY WITH YOUR OWN EYES!

They say about Santorini that that there is more wine here than water, there are more churches than houses, and there are more donkeys than people. All this is quite true in respect to Oia - a snow-white city in the north of Santorini. But only here is it still possible to find old mills, with which postcards with Oia's views are often decorated.

Oia is considered to be one of the most beautiful cities in Greece together with the capital of Santorini - Fira. In 1981, in Italy, it was even awarded the first prize of the European contest among the villages with the best traditional architecture.

One of the peculiar features of Oia is that here the magnificent view of the caldera of an extinct volcano is not spoiled by wires: all the power lines are conducted underground. The main observation deck of the city is located at its highest point, at the remains of the Venetian castle.

The city of Oia appeared on the map during the reign of the Turks in the late 16th - early 17th centuries, but received its name much later. Three centuries later, at the turn of the 19th – 20th centuries Oia flourished and became a city of sailors: the inhabitants had up to 130 ships with a total population of about 2,500 people.

After the earthquake in 1956, the city experienced a period of mass emigration, so that by 1977 only about 300 people were left to live here. Oia was returned to life due to a large-scale reconstruction, which turned a small island town into one of the most popular tourist destinations in the world.

Oia is primarily a city of newlyweds who come here from all over the world in order to get the most beautiful wedding photos. For them, even small separate houses are equipped here.

For many years, pairs of sweethearts from all over the world have been striving to Santorini to make an oath of love and loyalty in the magical atmosphere of an unusual island.

During the season, about 2,000 couples get married in Oia! An average wedding on Santorini costs from 20,000 Euros.

A legend says that a marriage, concluded on Santorini, will be strong and indestructible.

There are many options for the wedding ceremony. It can be a romantic wedding on a snow-white terrace in the background of the endless azure sea. Or an unforgettable evening in the Greek style, with lively dances. It is possible, secluded from the noise and fuss, to get spliced in a white and blue chapel under the rays of the setting sun. Or one can arrange a wedding on the deck of an old sailboat. And for fans of extreme, there is a possibility to exchange rings directly at the crater of the volcano. In any case, a wedding on the fabulous Santorini is going to be a bright and unforgettable event.

If you are just looking for privacy in a luxurious environment, then Oia is also perfect for such a holiday: in the evening on the terrace of your room neither the noise of cars nor the rumble of parties will prevent you from enjoying the silence; it's better to go to fashionable parties to Fira or some other resorts.

As on the whole island, the Mediterranean climate with hot sunny summer and mild rainy winter reign in Oia. Bathing season in Santorini opens in May and it lasts until October when the water still remains warmed up to +20 - +24°C. During the summer months, the air temperature stays stable around +30 - +35°C, in winter the air warms up to +10 - +12°C.

In all of Santorini, Oia is perhaps the most expensive city. High prices for accommodations are justified by the location of the hotels in about one line as an amphitheater and, accordingly, a chic view of the caldera and sunset from almost every room. Another characteristic feature of the hotels in Oia is that they are mainly small family-owned businesses with several rooms. In such boutique hotels, there are only 4-8 suites which are serviced at the highest level. Almost all of them have their own terrace; in addition, the hotels have an outdoor swimming pool.

In order not to go bankrupt at hotels (which at the same time are worth their money), it is better to choose accommodations from promotional offers of booking. So sometimes you can save up to 40-50% of the normal cost of accommodations. And of course, the rooms need to be booked in advance! Sometimes even 6-8 months in advance!

Oia on Santorini can hardly be considered the focus of attractions: like other cities of the island, as I said, Oia was seriously affected by the earthquake in 1956. But after the reconstruction, it turned into an architectural museum itself.

Oia is situated 11 km from Fira. There are small houses, located right at the edge of a sheer cliff, windmills, souvenir shops, and cozy taverns.

But there is a tourist attraction in Oia, because of which tourists all over the world dream to visit this small island village. It is the most beautiful sunset in the world, which can be observed from a certain place in Oia.

The sight of a fireball of the sun, slowly sinking into the blue waters of the sea, cannot be described in words; it only needs to be seen.

Seeing the sun in Oia turned into a beautiful tradition: having gathered on the ruins of the fortress, guests and residents of the island celebrate the disappearance of the star behind the horizon by applause, cries, kisses, hugs, and champagne on a day-to-day basis!

Below, at the foot of the rock, there are two beaches of Ammoudi and Armeni. The descent is very precipitous and very long. To get to the beaches you can only walk down the stairs with more than 200 steps.

If you nevertheless intend to diversify a measured rest by visiting interesting places, pay attention to the Maritime Museum, which stores parts of the surviving ships and instruments of seafarers, as well as thematic photographs and models of sea-going vessels.

The works of Modern Greek artists and sculptors are exhibited in the Art

Gallery of Oia, where you can not only admire the work of local authors, but also find an inexpensive and original souvenir.

Of the many churches scattered around the city, it is worth highlighting the church of St. Sozont, named after a shepherd who was executed by the emperor for sharing the Holy Scripture.

Oia. This is exactly the place from which more than a half of all the photographs on Santorini are made.

IMEROVIGLI

Famous for the whole world sceneries of Santorini, and snow-white houses with blue domes on the background of the endless sea, you will also find the town of Imerovigli, which is not far from the capital. These houses are in truth effectively decorated caves.

Imerovigli is a small town (village) 2 kms from the main city of Santorini, Fira, with stunning views of the sunsets, the volcano and the resort of Oia and with an incredibly dramatic history.

Not so long ago this resort was famous for the picturesque area of Scaros, which housed an ancient Venetian castle, wonderful mansions, and administrative buildings. However, the famous earthquake of 1956 sent the whole area down to the sea, turning it into a huge rock.

Along with the neighboring Firostefani, Imerovigli is one of the four main settlements in the caldera chain of Santorini between Fira and Oia. And although it is considered to be a relatively "quiet" direction of the island, do not expect that there won't be any people here.

Santorini is too small to be clearly manifested in the division into "large" and "medium" resorts. Once in the streets of Imerovigli, you will never say that there are only 470 permanent residents in the town. Imerovigli should be chosen as a place of basic accommodation on Santorini only if you want to avoid as much as possible the noisy crowds of tourists under the windows, but do not want to deprive yourself of such charms of civilization such as banks, shops, and museums.

Another advantage of Imerovigli in comparison with Fira and Oia is that when in the above-mentioned places there is nothing available for booking left, you can still find yourself a place to live here.

The houses of Imerovigli are stretched along the caldera, forming something similar to an amphitheater. By the way, this is very convenient for those who are looking for a good camera angle for a photo shoot.

You can get from Imerovigli to Fira on foot within 25-30 minutes.

FIROSTEFANI

Firostefani is a small village; the closest suburb of the capital of Santorini Island is Firo. Now it is a part of it.

Its name means "Crown of Fira." The village is not as crowded as the capital, which means it is an ideal place for a family holiday. Here you can eat well and tasty, see the magnificent sunset and enjoy the island.

There are many traditional streets. From the many parts of the city, there are delightful views of the volcano.

2. Transport

The buses often go to Santorini, and to almost all the interesting places of the island. This is very convenient; you can visit the attractions without renting a car or a quadricycle (on this Greek island such an option is also popular).

The buses on Santorini are based at a bus station, which is situated in the capital of the island, the city of Fira (Thira). There, most routes start and end; there is a ticket office where you can raise the burden of getting a ticket, buy tickets, and finding out the public transit schedules.

If you came to the island on a ferry, you can take a bus from the new port of Santorini to the city for 2.3 Euros per person. It is easy to find the buses: you will find them on the embankment a little further than all the greeters from the car and quadricycle renting agencies. Either number of the routes or names of the settlements will be written on the buses. As a rule, they all go to the Thira, but if you need to get to another village you should check with the conductor in place, as they will tell you everything.

In a large number of cases, the tickets are sold in a bus: on every route, there is a ticket collector who goes through the passenger compartment and gives out tickets.

You need to save tickets on the buses of Santorini till the end of the trip - on certain bus stops an inspector might get on a bus and he makes sure all the passengers have their tickets.

Bus stops on Santorini are not very noticeable. They do not have any signs, identification marks, names, or even any advertisements.

There are even simply small concrete fences, painted white on the background of concrete fences. Well, those stops where the main attractions are located, of course, stand out a little. For example, the stop near the black beach is also black).

The minimum bus fare is 1.8 Euros per person; the maximum one is 2.5 Euros. The highest bus fare on Santorini is on the routes of Fira – Vlychada, and Karterados - Vlychada.

For passengers with a large number of children (however, the number is not exactly specified), as well as passengers with disabilities, the cost of public transportation on Santorini is 50% lower.

For students, the discount for a ticket is 25%. Also, there is a night rate - from 00:30 to 05:00, the ticket price at this time is higher by 50-60 Euro Cents.

On Santorini's bus stops there are schedules of all the roundtrip bus routes. It is very convenient!

But, in the off-season, there is no need for the buses on Santorini to go so often. A few times I had to wait much longer than it was scheduled. But you can always specify the time of return trips by asking a conductor in the bus.

The public transport of the Santorini will take you to most of the sightseeing attractions of the island as quick as the wind.

Here are the most important sightseeing attractions: the city of Fira (Thira); the Oia city; Red Beach (Akrotiri) - and, in fact, the White Beach; black beach of Kamari; black beach of (Monolithos; black beach of Perissa; an exotic beach of Vlychada.

Also, buses to Santorini go from the bus station to the new port and to the airport.

Unfortunately, there are no maps of Santorini bus routes. Only local residents can help you to get to know how to go from point A to point B by bus. They will also show you the nearest bus stop.

You can also take a taxi or rent a car or a motorcycle on the island. It is better to go on foot throughout the cities or to use a traditional transport of Santorini – the donkeys.

It is better to order a car before your flight arrival (whether it is an airplane or a ferry) in advance, since there are few taxis on the island, and they mostly come to more efficient Greeks. Having ordered a car in advance, you will be sure that the car will come right up to you, and a driver will not be tempted by any other passengers.

Via two ports, Fira and Athenios (the main port), Santorini is connected by ferry service to Athens, Crete and other islands of Cyclades and Dodecanese. Numerous holiday cruisers and ships, which carry tourists to the beaches, the volcano, and to the rest of the islands of Santorini, also run from the ports.

Sea cruises to the uninhabited islands of Palea-Kameni, Nea-Kameni, and Aspronisi will help an insistent traveler to cover the entire archipelago, as well as walks throughout the peaceful Tyrasia, where one-day excursions start out from.

Petrol in Greece is expensive, so a taxi, especially on Santorini, is not cheap. I did not use taxi services, but this can be done on the island. But those who plan to use taxi services need to take not much more money!

3. Why do people go to Santorini?

On my deepest conviction, the most important thing in life is to create a strong family with a lot of kids and ... travel!

We should see all the beauty of the wonderful nature of our world with our own eyes. Each person should have a list of 10-20-30-100 =)) places that he should visit in his life.

The Greek islands (first of all, Santorini) must necessarily be at the top of this list.

So, why do people go to Santorini?

1. For the good of beautiful views of the caldera and an unforgettable sunset. This place is really magical and fairy tale enchanting, that is why people want to see all its beauty with their own eyes.

2. To carry out a wedding - a marriage ceremony. This place is fabulous. And any girl is a little princess at heart. Therefore, a wedding on this island is a dream for all the romantic couples from around the world. It is unforgettable to add a true fairy tale in real life!

3. The island is also famous for the fact that it is possible to seclude oneself in the wild. As they say, to find one's true identity. Forget about the fuss and think about the eternal. Here, as nowhere else, you can see and understand the power of nature and the price of time. Wise men, philosophers and those who like thinking about the essence of being will feel very comfortable here.

4. There is a category of people who choose this island, because of the night sky among other things. (I also belong to this category, for example.) Of course, one can say that the sky is the same from any part of the Earth, but true connoisseurs know that there are places in which the stars at night are shining unusually bright and mysteriously. The night sky is unforgettable, for example, in Madagascar or in the depths of the Sahara. The night sky on Santorini is also something from the realm of fantasy. Especially if you watch it from a small hot tub holding a glass of wine, in silence, on a small terrace of a cozy room, which is located at a height and is cut out right in the rock).

5. Food is delicious here! Food is really fantastic here because of the rich sun and volcanic soil. There are awesome wines and olive oil.

Of course, most people choose this place because of romance. It is everywhere. There is good news for shopping lovers, too. Practically all the brands are represented here as in Dubai. The choice of everything is just huge!

4. Beaches of Santorini

The volcanic beaches of Santorini are not inferior in popularity to the famous sunsets. There are about 20 places on the island where you can swim and sunbathe. The most well-known of them are Red Beach, Kamari, Perissa, and Vlychada beach.

On the beaches of Santorini, you can have a lot of fun at a disco, find oneself among the locals or be absolutely alone. Make your choice by the color of the sand or any other criteria which are important to you.

From the very beginning, it is worth noting that **people do not go to Santorini for the sake of beach holidays themselves. On other Greek islands, there are many comfortable, long beaches at lower prices. Beaches on Santorini are a tourist attraction.**

The eruption of the volcano, which occurred in 1450 BC., immersed the island into the sea and covered the rest with ashes; that is why the modern coastline has fancy outlines and colors. In the Western part of Santorini, a steep cliff with a height of 300 meters rises; it is not so easy to descend to the beaches as it is in the East, with its flat coastline. If you are going to Santorini for 2 or 3 days, then you'd better choose from the most popular and affordable beaches, as it is easy to combine visiting them with going sightseeing.

Perissa Beach

Perissa is one of the most famous beaches of Santorini.

It is located in a small village at the foot of Mount Mass Vuno, 15 kms from the capital of the island. You can get here by car, bus or water taxi.

It is covered with black volcanic sand. It is a very unusual sight. This is considered to be a visiting card of Santorini. The world's celebrities, including Hollywood stars, like to come by.

On this beach, there are comfortable sun loungers with mattresses and umbrellas to shield you from the sun. Here you can lie down to sunbathe even the whole day long or go in for water sports that are presented on the beach.

On this beach, there is a device for people with disabilities so that they can safely bathe in the sea as well.

In Perissa you can find the ruins of the old Byzantine church of St. Irene. Foreign pilgrims called this island "Santa Irini" and later Santorini.

Usually, this resort is chosen by elders. However, this beach is well suited for children to bathe, naturally, under the supervision of adults. The sea is crystal clear.

In Perissa, there is also the only water park on the island.

Due to the peculiarity of the sand, it heats up very much during the full blaze of the sun, so you need to walk on the beach with your shoes on. It is advisable that you go slowly in the water feeling the place where your foot goes.

The beach is well equipped, there is everything you need for a beach holiday, and there is a camping site nearby.

There are water entertainments such as scooters, catamarans, and parachutes. There are sun loungers at a reasonable price. There is parking nearby and it's free of charge. There is a shower and a changing room.

The length of the beach is 7 kms. The width of the beach strip is 30 ms. at an average.

Perissa, Perivolos, and Agios Georgios is a series of beaches with black sand, smoothly slipping one into another.

There is a diving center in Perissa. In the evening, the beach is beautifully lit; the active nightlife is humming with discotheques, DJs, and local and visiting celebrities.

On the beach of Perivolos, wedding ceremonies are often arranged.

Perivolos

Three kilometers from Perissa there is another popular beach, famous for its parties and bars - Perivolos.

Undoubtedly, it is one of the best beaches of Santorini.

In fact, this beach together with the beach of Agios Georgis is a continuation of the beach of Perissa.

This is a beach with the smallest black sand, along with the beach there is traditionally a great variety of bars and restaurants.

This is the favorite beach of the youth. It is the most comfortable beach and is deeply loved by the Greeks themselves. In the evenings, beach discos right in swimsuits and swimming trunks are arranged here.

It should be said that Greeks consider swimming trunks as what is considered to be shorts. And short man's swimming trunks can be associated among the Greeks with the non-traditional orientation of the owners of such swimming trunks.

The beach is separated from the city by a narrow path. Each beach area is served by a suitable cafe or a restaurant, to which the beach belongs. They also collect money for sun loungers and umbrellas. Sometimes you are not obliged to pay for sun loungers, just buy something to eat and drink in the same cafe.

The music sounds on the whole beach. Basically, these are dance rhythms.

The service has reached such a level that there are buttons on the sun umbrellas, by pushing them you can call a waiter, make or cancel an order, as well as ask for the bill.

Thus, in Perivolos, you can come in the morning, lie down on a sun lounger and spend the whole day on the beach ordering lunch right on the beach. In coastal cafes, the choice of dishes is also huge.

Many cafes have swimming pools and during the disco, you can dive into them or for example, dance with a bottle of beer in your hand.

The beach of Perivolos is best suited for relaxation and bathing with children.

Agios Georgios

Agios Georgios is a small resort village on Santorini, located 14 kms from Fira, the capital of the island. The resort is not very popular, so it will be an excellent solution for those who prefer to avoid noisy and crowded places. At the same time, here you will find all the attributes so familiar to resort settlements unless there are problems with transportation.

The beach of Agios Georgios is located at the very foot of the village. It is located just behind the beach of Perivolos (500 m. to the south) and it will be an ideal solution for those who want to spend a day on a spacious and uninhabited sea coast.

You can get to Agios Georgios from the village of Emborio (3 kms.) and Perissa (3.5 kms.) by taxi, rented car or moped. Buses do not go here, but with a great desire, you can walk on foot.

Around the coast, you will find many rooms and studios for rent, small motels, and hotels. Also here are a lot of various taverns and beach bars, and on top of that, there is a water sports center.

In the latter, by the way, you can go scuba diving, go water skiing, ride on a banana boat or practice windsurfing.

As for the coast itself, Agios Georgios can boast a picturesque black beach promenade (the result of the former volcanic activity of Santorini). On the shore, there are all the necessary conditions for recreation, such as sun loungers and umbrellas, as well as the coastal bars in walking distance.

Agios Georgios is the longest beach on Santorini. Also not far from Agios Georgios you will find an organized beach of Vlychada.

Red beach (Kokkini Paralia)

Red Beach ranks a special and honorable place among the best beaches of Santorini. Its name matches the color scheme. The correct name is Kokkini Paralia.

YOU MUST CERTAINLY VISIT THIS BEACH. YOU MUST TAKE A CAMERA BY ALL MEANS AND CAPTURE THIS BEAUTY BECAUSE YOU WILL NEVER SEE IT ANYWHERE ELSE.

This beach is unusual and of a rare beauty given to it by red pebbles in combination with the red color of the rocks towering above the beach.

It is located next to the archaeological excavations in Akrotiri. From the parking place of the car (a platform at the white church), you need to gently descend, making your way between the stones to reach the sea.

The beach is completely lined with sun loungers and umbrellas and is very quickly filled with people.

I knew it, so I came to Kokkini early in the morning. The red beach is surrounded by brick-red cliffs, on the shore and in the water, there are black and red porous pebbles. If the wind rises, towels and everything around gets covered with red sand.

Kamari

Kamari is located on a flat part of the island and is completely different from the precipitous part of Caldera. One gets an impression that this is not just another side, but completely another island.

Undoubtedly it is the most touristy-developed village of the island. A succession of the endless souvenir shops here alternates with the same number of cafes and coastal taverns.

Kamari beach is spacious; it is a mixture of black sand with black pebbles. Its length is 8 kms. up to the beach of Monolithos.

It is also equipped with sun loungers and umbrellas and bathes in the sun until 16:00 - 17:00, so it is more suitable for those who love sunbathing in the morning and in the afternoon or for those who like swimming late in the evening but cannot or do not want to stay in the sun.

They don't charge for sun loungers on the beach after 16:00 and it's great because this is the most favorable time for sunbathing as there's less harm to the skin.

Kamari beach with its black sand was awarded the Blue Flag. Direct buses from Fira, the capital of Santorini, go to Kamari. At this popular resort, there is a promenade along the sea, restaurants, shops and water attractions.

When I was swimming, I hurt my knee painfully on the stone bottom. It is said that natural stone slabs do not lie everywhere. The sea deepens after 2 or 3 meters. Such a dive into the water, of course, is not fit for children.

But this resort is very popular among those who rest with children. For them, there is a separate well-developed territory with attractions, where professional animators work with children. The child, in general, may be left with them for half a day while you go somewhere to have fun. For example, fans of archeology will be interested in seeing the ruins of the ancient city of Fira. To do this, you will need to climb from the village of Kamari to the top of the mountain of Mesa vouno (400 ms.). Ancient Fira was founded in the 9th century BC. Until now, the remains of the temple of Dionysus, the ancient agora, and the royal gallery, the shrine of Apollo, the ancient theater, and traces of Byzantine churches have been preserved.

In many hotels in Kamari, entertainment representatives work with small tourists as well.

In general, the beach adds to the impressions of visiting the volcanic island.

Kamari is an excellent resort of high quality, but for fans of nightlife, it can be quite boring. It is better for such people to go to the capital of the island.

In Kamari, people walk around the shops or have dinner while listening to pleasant and quiet music in the coastal cafes in the evenings. This is a great place for connoisseurs of evening rest and relaxation accompanied by the quiet whisper of waves on the beach.

Translated from Greek, Kamari means pride. I'm sure you will also be proud if you spend your vacation here.

In this resort, in the evenings you can enjoy quiet whisper of waves on the beach merging with the starry night sky.

Going to the resort of Kamari, do not forget to visit the Wine Museum, where you will not only be treated with a local-made drink, but will also be shown a cave for storing bottles at a depth of 300 meters. The Museum has an audio guide practically in all the languages. At one time the island was the main Greek wine supplier to France.

<u>Monolithos Beach</u>

Translated from Greek, Monolithos means a monolith. The beach was named so because of the lonely rock standing here. This is also a black beach. There is real peace here. Hotels and restaurants are located at a distance from each other, that is why you can wander long and all by yourself along the strip of beach washed by the oncoming turquoise waves, and white foam that creates an ineffable contrast with the black sand of the beach. What an amazing place!

It is here that you can find real volcanic foam! Yes, it's that volcanic foam we rub the heels with. These are white stones of volcanic origin. Here's a great souvenir for you from the island. By the way, local people sell similar pebbles in souvenir shops for 1-2 Euros.

On the same beach, you can even find pieces of cooled lava. There are round black porous pebbles, from which the resourceful Greeks make statuettes or ornaments, and sell them at a rather expensive price.

Next to this beach, there is Santorini Airport. Free entertainment is watching the landing and taking off of the airplanes. By the way, you can spend time waiting for your flight on this beach.

The beach is sandy with a shallow approach to the water and it is well-developed, that is why it's suitable for recreation with children. You can rent a sun lounger and an umbrella or sit in the shade of a tree.

It is a quiet place with a beautiful view of the volcano and the sunset.

In the evenings there is nothing to do at this resort unless your hotel holds some recreational activities. You can rent a car and get acquainted with the island.

The main disadvantage of this beach of Santorini is that if the wind rises, then it's not quite comfortable to stay here, because clouds of sand are pouring out into the air. The good thing is that it doesn't happen very often.

Other visited beaches of Santorini

Akrotiri Caldera Beach

This small beach is not very wide (about 8 meters) with black sand and a good way into the water. It is located under the caldera near the village of the same name. There is a diving center nearby, you can dip in the water or dive with a mask. The water is clean and clear. The beach offers magnificent views of Fira, the Old Port, and even Oia, looking out from behind the Stone in the center of the caldera.

But an unusual color is, perhaps, the only advantage of this beach. In the low season, the waves are constantly rising, so it is simply impossible to swim here.

In summer all the coast is covered with sun loungers so that there isn't enough room to swing a cat: the beach is quite small, let me remind you. Furthermore, this beach is more often than not closed for visiting because of the rock falls. Therefore, a large number of tourists come here only to take some photos of the beach with brick-red rocks from the top of the mountain and to have a walk here and there on the sand of such an unusual color. It is rather a quiet place with a beautiful view of the volcano and the sunset.

In Akrotiri, you can find excavations of ancient settlements.

The settlement of the Minoan period, discovered in 1967 by chance, became one of the most important archaeological discoveries in the world. The buildings and objects were perfectly preserved due to the thick layer of volcanic ash. The ancient city of Akrotiri was an important trade center, rich and prosperous until the eruption of the volcano ceased its existence.

In addition to excavations in Akrotiri, you can see the churches of the Holy Trinity and the Holy Mother, as well as the Venetian castle. It's 3 kms from the village, and on the westernmost point of the island, there is a lighthouse from which a wonderful view opens.

White beach. Aspri Paralia

Secluded from Fira on 14 km, it is a beach with white sand and white rocks surrounding it.

Almost all beaches of Santorini can be reached by bus or rented transport. The exception is the White Beach of Santorini. You can get here only by boat from the port of Akrotiri for 5 Euros per person. Any hotels on this beach, of course, are out of the question.

That's why the White Beach is the most romantic and secluded on the island. There are few tourists here even in the highest season, there are no clubs and restaurants, only umbrellas, sun loungers, and a food cart. And there are snow-white rocks, the shore at the foot of which is strewn with the pebbles of the same color.

But the entrance to the sea on the White Beach is not very comfortable - large stones are replaced by stone slabs there. But this inconvenience is more than compensated by a wonderful landscape, which you will not see anywhere else.

The most romantic beach of Santorini, the photos of which are not able to reflect the greatness of the white rocks and blue water will be appreciated by couples in love. Choose comfortable shoes to explore the caves of the White Beach and just to walk easily on the sand and the large stones covering the coast.

Vlychada beach

It is a secluded place near Perivolos, 13 kms from Fira, in the southernmost part of Santorini.

Here everything resembles the planet Mars. There is a beach with black sand. Sensations are cosmical. The rocks resemble the lunar surface; an unusual landscape is complemented by two pipes of the former brick factory. Private yachts are moored in Vlychada Bay, and there is the Sailing & Yachting Center.

Vlychada is a really beautiful beach!!! Many people consider this very beach to be the most wonderful beach on Santorini. A wide beach line, black shining sand (looks similar to caviar), the minimum number of tourists (and sometimes the total absence of tourists) aren't the main advantages of this beach. To the top of my rating of "The best beaches of Santorini" Vlyhada was put due to sheer cliffs along the coastline, over which the great sculptor, the wind has been working for centuries, decorating them from the bottom to the top with bizarre patterns in the genre of abstract art.

And thanks to these rocks there are no hotels near Vlychada, because of this fact there are always a few people here. Several hotels are situated only at the very beginning of this beach. There are a few sun loungers with umbrellas. All the rest of Vlychada is free from any beach innovations and it is at your full disposal, and only sometimes your unity with nature will be violated by the cough of elderly nudists, the presence of which have become a side effect of almost all the beautiful beaches of Greece.

The beach is quiet; the nudists sunbathe on the right side. If you want to get to secluded and inaccessible bays in the South of the island, it makes sense to buy a tour of the beaches of Santorini, and you will be transported by boat.

Basically, such tours start in Fira, Kamari or Perissa, from where the bus leaves. Boarding a boat in Vlychada Bay, then cruising to Faros - a lighthouse and a rock in the shape of an Indian head, a stop on the Lovers Beach, White Beach, Red Beach, bus stop in Vlychada and return. Such beach tours are designed for 5-6 hours, including stops for swimming and the road.

Eros

The beach of Eros, 6 kms long and 35 meters wide, is situated in the south and is considered one of the most glamorous holiday destinations on Santorini.

They say that nudists can often be seen here, but they are rather difficult to find - apparently they prefer to remain unnoticed.

A quiet and tranquil beach, protected from strong winds by a high hill, provides for relaxation. There aren't any noisy restaurants and bars here, only huge umbrellas, comfortable chaise lounges, dark gray sand, an unusual relief of rocks and a reunion with nature. If you want to have a snack, you can go up a little higher and look into the tavern, which offers dishes of Mediterranean cuisine. The water is blue, clean and transparent, but sharp stones near the shore slightly spoil the impression of bathing. You can get to Eros only in a rented car, and then leave it on a parking lot neighboring the beach.

Other beaches

(These beaches are suitable for lovers of secluded holidays)

Ammoudi Bay

It is located near the village of Oia, from where 260 stairs lead to Ammoudi Bay. The bay can be reached by car and then you walk for 5 minutes. It is famous for its clear water, and it's suitable for diving.

Paradisos

Raradisos Beach or Paradise Beach is located in a short drive from Oia.

It will be ingratiating for those who seek peace and are ready to give up some of the benefits of the civilization. In a season on a coastal strip covered with black and gray sand with impregnations of small pebbles, sun loungers and umbrellas are set.

The sea is shallow near the coast, but large rocks complicate the entrance to clean water. Like other beaches of Santorini, Paradisos is surrounded by restaurants, snack bars, and taverns.

It's a good beach for families with children, located next to Oia on the other side of the island with a view of the sunrise.

Pori

This beach is popular with locals. There are rocks of red color, beautiful views of the bay, mills, and sunset. This is not the best place for swimming, there are no sun loungers and umbrellas, but there is local charm and tranquility.

Vourvoulos

This beach is located in the north-eastern part of Santorini, 7 kms from Fira.

Sand-and-pebble coastal strip of dark gray color (sometimes saturated black), turquoise water and complete isolation contribute to a vacation away from the hustle and bustle.

It's nice to stroll along the beach and make picnics at a safe distance from the surf line, the sea sometimes storms and waves raise because of the winds.

The rest of the time Vourvoulos is a quiet beach for surfing without sun loungers and umbrellas, but with a small restaurant.

It's a quiet non-tourist place. With a strong wind, large waves raise on the beach.

Katharos

Katharos is located next to the city of Oia, which makes it an ideal choice for those who are staying in the north-western part of Santorini and do not want to travel long distances for a swim.

The black pebble beach of Katharos, surrounded by high cliffs, cannot boast of providing public amenities.

Of the amenities, there is only a smooth entry into the sea, but many visitors come here for the love of the Katharos Lounge restaurant.

They say that this place on the beach offers the best food not only on Santorini but throughout Greece.

Kambia Beach

This beach is located in the south-west of Santorini, between Mesa Pigadia and the Red Beach. You can get there by car; you'd better take an offroadster since the road to the beach is hard riding. Not far from the beach there are two churches and a picturesque cave.

Kambia is reliably hidden from the winds by coastal rocks and strewn with large pebbles. On foreseeingly set sun loungers, in the shade of large umbrellas you can hide from crowds of tourists, and in a typical Greek tavern you can try a simple, but delicious meal.

Baxedes Beach

Baxedes Beach is an ideal option for those who want to avoid excessively busy beaches, make many beautiful photos and fully enjoy the atmosphere of Santorini and Greece. Baxedes with a narrow coastal strip, a mixture of black sand, small pebbles and large stones is located 3 kms from Oia.

The entry to the sea is convenient, but the depth starts right off the coast, and due to the northern winds, high waves rise, so the beach is not recommended for older people and families with children. The rest of the visitors are provided with an acquaintance with untouched nature, renting everything necessary for recreation and having a pleasant time in a local tavern.

Koloumbos

It is a small beach in ten minutes' walk from Baxedes. The road to the "secret" place is surrounded by rocks and bottomless canyons. On the way, you can see a small church - white, with a blue dome like many others in Santorini. Earlier, Koloumbos with dark pebbles and underwater volcano undividedly belonged to nudists; today everyone can relax on this beach, but it remains a little crowded because of undeveloped infrastructure, which only adds to its natural charm.

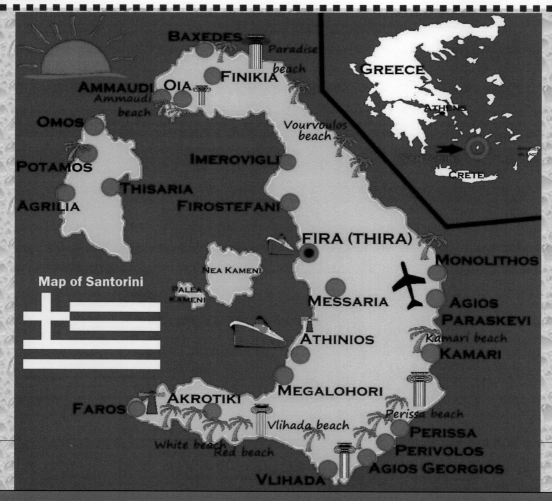

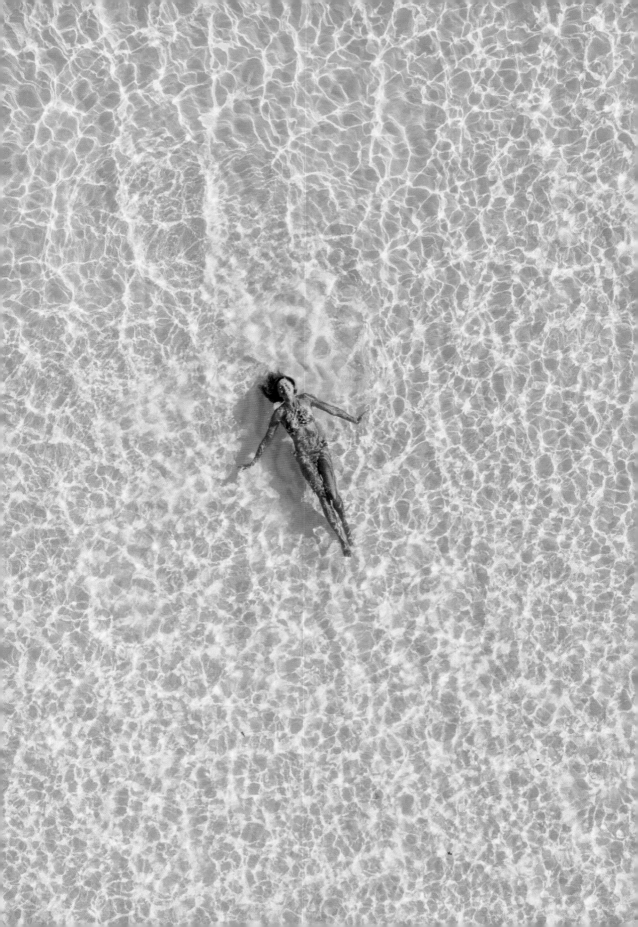

5. Hotels

Hotels on Santorini overlooking the caldera of the volcano are a real decoration of this Greek island. As a rule, such hotels are built on the slope of the cliff, and some of them are even carved into a rock or a cave. They are so picturesque that many tourists take pictures of them, even without realizing that in fact, they are taking photos of the hotels.

It is not surprising that Santorini hotels with a view of the caldera are considered to be the most prestigious on the island. Spending the evening, not in the crowd of tourists, but on your own terrace or in the pool instead, admiring the sunset against on the background of the sea with a glass of wine in your hand, this is a special chic. **And this is what you absolutely must do!**

That is why the prices for Santorini hotels, which have a view of the caldera of the volcano, are usually higher than the average on the island. However, among these prestigious hotels, there are quite inexpensive ones (if compared with an average price for such hotels).

Almost all Santorini hotels, overlooking the caldera, are located in three cities: Fira, Imerovigli, and Oia, in each of these towns (villages).

The number of hotels in these places is huge. I advise you to look through as many options as possible so that you would not miss the one that best suits you.

There are some options that, in my opinion, deserve your attention. Of those hotels that are more expensive, pay attention to the following (but be sure to check out some other options).

Ikies - Traditional Houses
Anastasis Apartments
Aenaon Villas
Astra Suites
Andronis Boutique Hotel
Pezoules
Enigma Apartments & Suites
The Vasilicos
Celestia Grand
Artemis Villas
Andronis Luxury Suites
Anteliz Suites
Canaves Oia Sunday Suites
Kapari Natural Resort

Below is a list of in expensive hotels you should pay attention to, but again I recommend you look through more options that can be easily found on the Internet.

Santorini Hostel
Santorini Camping/Rooms
Lignos (two-star hotel)
Porto Castello
Hotel Hellas (two-star hotel)
Villa Ilios
Marousi Rooms
Museo Grand Hotel
Emmanouela Studios & Villas
Villa Clio

Search some information about these hotels at the official websites, as well as on the well-known sites for finding hotels.

There you can find out about prices, see some photos of the rooms, read real tourists' reviews and book a room.

6. What to do on Santorini?

There can be hundreds of answers to this question - from tasting the local wine to bathing in sulfur spring-wells. Though tourists usually come here for a short period of time, they want to succeed in so many things! Therefore, I will tell you about 5 things that every tourist should do. So, what to do in Santorini so that you could take the maximum of impressions from here?

1. To meet the sunset in Oia

Of the many options for what to do on Santorini, most tourists put on the first place meeting of the sunset in Oia. Every evening crowds of tourists come together, and they arrive and sail to the north of the island of Santorini. They have a common goal - to take beautiful photos of the sunset on Santorini, and they have a general direction - the village of Oia.

Most of these tourists have a common gathering place - the ruins of the Venetian fortress. It is the very place from which **opens the best view** of the bright red ball of the Sun in Oia, slowly drowning in the Aegean Sea against the background of the surrounding islands.

2. To visit the excursion on the volcano

The eruptions of volcanoes in their time raised two small islands of Nea Kameni and Palea Kameni from the sea depths, which now stick out in the middle of the caldera and which tourists admire at sunset from Fira and Oia. The islands are completely lifeless, uninhabited and covered with black stones with sand. Both of them are strewn with craters, from which the clouds of romantic yellow smoke still burst forth. It is unusual and beautiful, but very creepy.

Since you came to Santorini, the tour of the volcano must necessarily be on your program. The price of such trips starts from 20-30 Euros and includes visits to the island of Nea Kameni (a walk around the volcano) and Palea Kameni (bathing in hot springs near the island). For some extra charge, you can upgrade the program by visiting the island of Tirasia, meeting the sunset at sea and other options.

On the island of Nea Kameni you will find burned down, the lifeless land dotted with black ash and stones, from under which clouds of the smoke break out... and near the island of Palea Kameni you can bathe in hot sulfur springs. The closer to the shore, the warmer the water becomes and the more rust-colored are the swimsuits. And for the dessert, you will find the island of Tirasia waiting for you with its fish restaurants.

3. Relax on the black beaches

On Santorini, as you already know, there are different colored beaches: black, red and white. But not all the people have a desire to visit the last two beaches. Anyway, you should definitely have a look at the black beaches of Santorini, covered with volcanic sand. And not only should you have a look, but also spend a day or two there. As already mentioned, there are three main black beaches on Santorini. Vlychada is the most beautiful, Perissa is the longest and Kamari ... is simply Kamari. If there is no time to see all three of them, then be sure to visit Vlychada; in addition to silvery black sand, this beach will surprise you with a bizarre pattern which an invisible sculptor has been cutting out on the local rocks for centuries.

4. To ride donkeys

Long ago, when Santorini was not one of the most popular islands in the world, the main means of transportation here were donkeys. You may go up from the port of Santorini to the town as I said riding a donkey. Therefore, do not deny yourself such a pleasure, especially since it costs only 5 Euros!

5. Walking from Fira to Oia

This is not an easy task, I warn you.

Yes, Fira, the capital of the island is as much as 11 kms from the elite village of Oia. Yes, the route passes not only along convenient tracks, but also winds up and down along the paths laid by your predecessors on lifeless volcanic ash. But after all, what is Santorini? These are neat white houses with blue shutters, blue domes of churches and beautiful views of the caldera of the volcano. All this is plenteously waiting for you on the route from Fira to Oia, and there are just crazy views of the caldera!

I advise you to set off four hours before sunset, and at the end point of your walk in reward for the efforts, you will receive the most magical sunset in the world. (Shoes during this walk should be comfortable and lasting!)

6. To visit the traditional Greek villages such as Imerovigli, Pyrgos, Megalohori and Emporio.

In the traditional Greek villages, in my opinion, the real soul of Greece is hiding. People are very friendly and hospitable. Their unfeigned sincerity is felt by the heart. These gray grandfathers and old grandmothers are happy to see you as if they are your relatives and they treat you like a friend, not like a tourist. It is very pleasant.

7. Food.

Features and secrets of the national Greek cuisine

On Santorini, everything is not only beautiful, but also very tasty.

Greeks love and most importantly know how to cook, turning national Greek dishes into a work of art. It is a fact.

The unique soil of the island allows growing delicious vegetables, famous throughout Greece.

From the local cuisine, of course, try seafood caught in the surrounding waters.

Be sure to try the local delicacies - white eggplants, roasted on coals and sprinkled with grated cheese.

Domatoceftedes are cutlets of the small but sweetest tomatoes (salty and very juicy).

Fava is a special kind of peas. It is the puree of local beans of the same name. This puree is similar to pasta and it should be spread on local bread (preferably while it's still hot).

And for dessert try cherry tomato jam, or traditional cookies with cottage cheese called Meletinya.

Do not miss a chance to try the products of local winemakers. Produced from ancient varieties of grapes (only one plant survived in the layer of volcanic ash, the grape-vine), Santorini's wine is mysterious, like the island itself. Even the vineyards are unusual: the grape-vine is laid in a shape of a basket near the ground to protect the racemations from the north wind.

The most famous local wine is the light white Asirtico, the aged white Nichteri, and of course, the famous Vincanto, which is thick, sweet, velvet wine filled with the aroma of honey. Vinsanto is made of sun-dried grapes and is prepared in oak barrels. Personally, I liked Espirico the most.

I highly recommend that you drink this wine after all the local food you eat.

I believe that Greek cuisine is one of the most delicious cuisines in the world and at the same time it might be the best for your health.

For the first time, I experienced real Greek cuisine at Crete. I was delighted with her taste and I did not believe that the products I had known earlier could be far more delicious than usual. I could not understand the secret. The secret as it turned out really exists. It's all about the products grown in Crete.

They have twice stronger taste owing to the location of the island. Crete is the southernmost island of Greece and the products grown here by local residents receive a double dose of sun. Thus, traditional Greek dishes cooked from products grown in Crete, acquire distinctive, simply divine taste. Such dishes should be tasted at the local cafes in tiny traditional villages lost in the depths of the island.

So, let's get back to Santorini. Imagine the taste of the products that are grown in Santorini, under the generous sun and also in volcanic soil.

I belong to the fans of the Greek cuisine and I am sure that after visiting the Greek islands you will also become fans of this cuisine.

Features of national Greek cuisine

National dishes of Greek cuisine are distinguished by rich shades of taste and usefulness. Many nutritionists recommend that you follow a Mediterranean diet based on the principles of Greek cuisine for weight normalization.

The benefits of Greek national cuisine are determined by simple but important factors:

1. Use of healthful products - fresh vegetables, greens, made in-house cheese, seafood, fruit;

2. Greeks do not use fast food excessively;

3. The most popular and traditional product is olive oil, which is added to many dishes of national cuisine, its healthfulness has been known for thousands of years;

4. National dishes are seasoned with lemon juice instead of salt; citrus fruit is added to the main dishes (meat and fish), marinades, and desserts;

5. Greeks often use lots of dairy products such as yoghurt, goat milk, feta, and brinsen cheese.

The main feature of the national cuisine is natural, environmentally friendly products; most are grown and produced in the country.

It should be noted that according to statistics, Greeks are less likely to get heart and oncological pathologies and obesity. The first book on the Greek food culture was written in 330 BC.

Recommendations

While on Santorini or on other Greek islands, you are obliged to try:

From the main courses:

"Fasolada" - traditional bean soup;

"Fakes" - lentil soup with an addition of salted fish, cheese (mostly brinsen cheese), olives and red onions. These kinds of soup are offered in hot weather.

In winter in the menu of restaurants there are richer and more nourishing kinds of soup:

"Avgolemono" - soup with rice grits and chicken broth with a whipped egg and lemon juice;

"Vrasto" is national beef soup.

Snacks

Traditionally, every meal begins with snacks that stimulate the appetite. They are served in small diameter bowls. Snack foods, which are loved by the Greeks themselves, are the following:

"Dzadziki" is both a snack and a sauce made from yoghurt, fresh cucumbers, olive oil, and fragrant garlic;

"Dolmadakya" is an appetizer from rice, minced meat, wrapped in leaves of grapes;

"Kalamarakya" - roasted calamary;

"Taramasalata" - a national dish of smoked codfish caviar, olives, greens, a lemon and vegetable oil;

"Tirokaftery" - a traditional soft cheese snack of pepper (spicy sorts).

Salads

"Melidzanosalata" is a hot salad, a mixture of baked eggplants, vegetable oil, spices, lemon, and fragrant garlic. Sometimes yogurt and tomatoes are added to the dish, seasoned with green onions. Dietitians consider this dish is beyond reproach in terms of the principles of proper nutrition, and gourmets rightfully consider this combination of products to have the pure taste.

"Greek salad" contains tomatoes, cucumbers, sweet peppers, onions, olives, flavored spices and olive oil, complemented with feta cheese. You probably will be interested in trying a Greek salad in its homeland.

"Lahano" is a salad of white cabbage, carrots, celery roots and leaves; some housewives add sweet pepper into the salad.

Meat dishes

The culture of the national Greek cuisine is based on one fundamental rule –

there is no need to complicate things. A good dish, according to the Greeks, is cooked as quickly and easily as possible, which is why meat is simply baked in any convenient way.

Traditional Greek meat dishes are:

• "Brizoles" - juicy, fragrant meat on the bone;

• "Suvlaki" - compact shashlyk;

• "Paidakia" - traditionally baked ribs (usually lambs);

What should the admirers of European cuisine taste in Greece?

"Bifteks" are ordinary chopped cutlets of different diameters, seasoned with aromatic herbs, cheese, and various vegetables.

National traditions of Greek cuisine are based on the culture of many peoples, for many decades they were formed under the influence of the Turkish oppression:

"Suzukakia" - traditional cutlets, thickly seasoned with spices;

"Kebabs" - a masterful dish which is prepared in the northern regions, where the Turkish diaspora settled down.

Treats of national Greek cuisine, which must be tried, are:

• "Kuneli" - rabbit meat stewed with vegetables;

• "Arni lemonato" - lamb meat cooked with lemon marinade;

• "Kokonisto" - beef meat with tomato marinade;

• "Pastitio" - puff pastry made of pasta, minced meat, traditional white marinade.

Garnish is served to meat - some rice and vegetables.

Fish dishes

What food to taste in Greece? Every tourist will definitely answer this question, - fish and, of course, seafood. Original Greeks residents highly esteem the gifts of the sea because the state is located on the coast of the sea.

Large fish, baked on charcoal or grilled, is seasoned with vegetable oil and lemon juice.

Small fish like sea tongue, surmullet, and red mullet is fried. Also, they most commonly fry cod, stingray, swordfish, and shark (a small one, Mediterranean).

The traditional approach to cooking involves the flawless freshness of the products. The price is determined by the place of catching; the local fish costs more than the imported one. The fish menu in restaurants is more expensive than the meat one.

Popular dishes:

• Octopus: baked or boiled;

• Calamary: traditional baked - "Kalamaria Tiganita," fried with a cheese filling - "Kalamaria Jemista me Thiri";

• Cuttlefish stewed with spinach leaves;

• Shrimps: fried or stewed in tomato-cheese marinade;

• Traditional mussels steamed or cooked in the tomato-cheese marinade.

<u>Signature national dish in the Greek cuisine is lobster with the pasta called "Makaronada me Astako."</u>

Gifts of the sea are given special attention; culinary masterpieces are cooked from them, which will easily enchant a discerning gourmet. If you want to try something special, pay attention to a shrimp dish, cooked in tomato sauce and seasoned with feta cheese, or to an octopus dish in sweet wine, seasoned with spices.

Desserts

Traditional sweet dishes of Greek cuisine are, above all, Turkish heritage. By the way, the tradition of drinking coffee, prepared in a jezve, also remains from the Ottoman Empire.

Having a rest on Santorini or other Greek islands, be sure to please yourself with original desserts:

• "Lukumades" - balls made from dough, seasoned with spices, poured with honey, and sprinkled with powdered sugar;

• "Pakhlava" - a traditional pie filled with fruit syrup, chopped walnuts; the dessert, as a rule, is prepared with 33 layers (the symbol of the age of Christ);

• "Kurabedes" - shortbread cookies with almonds;

• "Rizogalo" - pudding from rice, dried fruits, nuts, and seasoned with cinnamon;

• "Halvas" - halva, which is prepared of semolina.

Greek sauces

If you are studying Greek dishes that you need to taste during a trip, be sure to pay attention to the sauces. The Greeks have a perfect clue about them and cook them for almost every dish. Features of traditional Greek sauces are:

- Only natural ingredients;

- No complex recipes;

- Maximum healthiness.

The main principle of the right sauce is that it should delicately emphasize the taste and aroma of the main treat.

The ingredients of the sauce should be as universal as possible and be combined with fish, seafood, meat, and vegetables. Most often in the cooking process is used:

- Vegetable (olive) oil;

- Lemon juice;

- Natural yoghurt;

- Special Greek garlic.

The classic sauce is "Avgolemono." It is served with main courses and salads, and it's used in cooking soups. It takes only a few minutes to prepare it, a mixture of eggs and lemon juice is watered down with broth. Proportions are selected individually depending on the desired thickness of the sauce. The marinade gives the main dish a slightly sour taste.

There is a secret of cooking - you cannot bring the marinade to the boil, as the egg white will curl up.

For seafood, they prepare marinade from mustard, vegetable oil, lemon juice, and a mixture of dried herbs. In some regions, honey is added to this mixture, it gives the dish a soft, smooth texture. For fish and as a salad dressing they prepare a sauce of only two components - lemon juice and olive oil.

The main dishes are served with "Skorthalia" sauce, made from fragrant garlic, almonds and vegetable oil. Sometimes in the sauce breadcrumbs and finely chopped potatoes are added. So you get a rich snack.

There is a secret of cooking - to avoid the strong taste of garlic, it is pre-baked.

Original sauce "Fava" is cooked from beans or lentils puree, seasoned with olive oil, lemon juice, natural yogurt and herbs (usually parsley).

Food of national production

Greek cheese deserves a special mention. The country produces more than 60 sorts of cheese, each of which is served as a snack or main dish, used for cooking other dishes. During your stay in Greece, I recommend you to try such kinds of cheese:

• "Feta" - white cheese, tough enough, made of sheep's milk (less often of goat's milk).

• "Gravier" - cheese of sweet taste, hard consistency, made of sheep's milk.

• "Manuri" - sheep cheese with a soft, delicate texture, high caloric content.

• "Casserie" - cheese of a mixture of sheep and goat's milk, white, with a light yellowish shade.

• Kefalotiri - spicy cheese with a salty flavor and a solid, porous structure.

Another traditional dish is olive oil. Here it is sold in every grocery store. Sometimes you can try the product before purchasing. Oil is presented in its pure state or with an addition of spices, and fragrant herbs.

National drinks

Ouzo

The most famous alcoholic Greek drink is ouzo. It's worth trying in the first place.

Ouzo is prepared by distillation of alcohol with the addition of anise, a bouquet of spices (most often - cinnamon, nutmeg, and cloves). On the territory of Greece there are many manufacturers of this beverage, so the composition and percentage of alcohol content may differ - from 20% to 40%.

Ouzo is used with fish dishes and seafood; it is served in tall, narrow glasses. In grocery stores, the drink is sold in bottles of different volumes; the minimum cost is 3 Euros.

Tsipuro and raki

Tsipuro and raki are alcoholic beverages with an alcohol content of 37% to 47%, which resemble home-distilled vodka. The main difference between them is the presence of anise – it is present in tsipuro, but there is no spice in raki.

Tsipuro is served chilled, in a decanter with a high, narrow bottleneck. The beverage is drunk from small glasses, in one gulp. As a rule, tsipuro is ordered by the Greeks of the older generation, the younger generation prefers other drinks. The cost of one bottle varies from 4 to 5 Euros.

Rakomelo

This is an alcoholic beverage, which consists of two components - honey and raki (the one described above). Sometimes they add cinnamon and cloves. This drink is often cooked in a cold season because you need to drink it hot. Some Greeks use rakomelo as a remedy for a cold.

Rakomelo can be bought in any supermarket, but it is better to do-it-yourself: buy some raki and honey. The process takes several minutes, and the taste is much better than the store product. Pour raki into a jezve, heat it up, add some honey according to your taste, and remove from the fire before boiling. The drink is ready, now you can try it!

Metaxa

The liquor of Greek production, its distinctive feature is the presence of mastic - resin, which is obtained from the evergreen shrub. Mastic in Greece is used for cooking many dishes, as well as in cosmetology.

The liqueur is served as an aperitif and after a meal for better digestion. The taste of mastic is original and memorable, sweetish, with a light fruity-coniferous aroma. The price of one bottle is about 10 Euros.

Coffee

A very popular drink in Greece is coffee. It seems that it is drunk constantly - hot, cold, with foam and without it, with milk or cream, with the addition of various spices. Probably only those who have some health problems do not drink coffee in Greece.

If you want to fully understand what the national Greek dishes are, try them not in the hotel, but in the local taverns and restaurants. This is the only way you can feel the taste of the real Greece!

Prices for food in restaurants and cafes on Santorini are more expensive than in other islands of Greece. In those places where the sunset is seen best, the prices in restaurants and cafes are correspondingly even higher. But there is good news, mostly in all cafes and restaurants are very large portions. A lot of tourists order food for one person and this is enough to eat well for two. The average cost of dinner or dinner is very different.
Can be from 40 to 60 euros per person.

8. Conclusion

Santorini is an amazing island. Everything is amazing and romantic here! Here, you look differently at things which seemed ordinary, and you find something unusual in them.

Especially charming is the morning's fresh and almost cool breeze with the singing of birds and the ringing of bells. Fabulous seems the night with an incredible starry shine.

Views from the height to the depths of the sea and volcanoes simply shock the mind.

You will take an unforgettable experience with you from this island. And as souvenirs, you can buy, for example, jewelry in special jewelry stores, as Greece is famous for its jewelry masters.

In Fira, right in the street, a guy draws very funny and beautiful comical pictures; this is also an original souvenir.

Well, among the traditional souvenirs there certainly are different magnets, pieces of volcanic foam, jewelry items, perfume soap, and olive oil.

For religious people, it will be useful to buy little local icons.

The best time to visit the island is the period from early May to October. In winter the island is practically empty.

Many people come here just for one day to see the sunset. I recommend that you spend at least 3 nights here.

In general, it will be optimal to stay on the island of Crete during your holiday. This is the largest island in Greece and is also simply beautiful. It is full of attractions. And then from Crete, you can go to Santorini on the ferry for at least 3 days.

In conclusion, I want to emphasize that life on Santorini is not hasty. Everywhere reins harmony and tranquility.

Santorini really takes one's breath away with its beauty and yet one can't get rid of a feeling that there is something unreal in this place, it seems that this is a dream of a day-dreamer, embodied among the blue waters. The magic of this place makes you dizzy. If you really want to see a dream in reality, come to Santorini at least once. I ask you to come! Believe me; the impressions from this unearthly beauty you'll get after visiting this island will warm your soul with the memories for the rest of your life!

The residents of Santorini say that you can really appreciate their island only when you've left it. Maybe that's why everyone who has visited the magical Santorini, dreams of a new journey to this corner of paradise in the Mediterranean!

Printed in Great Britain
by Amazon